Ready for your love

Ready for your love
And other poems

Kwami E. Nyamidie

iUniverse, Inc.
New York Lincoln Shanghai

Ready for your love
And other poems

All Rights Reserved © 2004 by Kwami E. Nyamidie

No part of this book may be reproduced or transmitted in any form or by any means, graphic, electronic, or mechanical, including photocopying, recording, taping, or by any information storage retrieval system, without the written permission of the publisher.

iUniverse, Inc.

For information address:
iUniverse, Inc.
2021 Pine Lake Road, Suite 100
Lincoln, NE 68512
www.iuniverse.com

ISBN: 0-595-30643-8

Printed in the United States of America

Consciousness, oh consciousness, why do you leave me at night?

YOU'RE IT
God
Disguised
As a myriad things and
Playing a game
Of tag
Has kissed you and said
"You're it—
I mean, you're Really it!"
Hafiz. 1999. *The Gift*. Ladinsky, D. (Translator). New York: Penguin. p. 30.

Contents

PART I   LOVERS PLAY HIDE AND SEEK

A lover getting ready 3
All I want is love, love, love 4
Ineffable love 7
Numinous lovers play hide and seek (1) 9
Numinous lovers play hide and seek (2) 10
Numinous lovers play hide and seek (3) 11
Numinous lovers play hide and seek (4) 12
Committing to Spirit 13
Compassion 16

PART II   EGG IN A TORNADO EYE

You all are in my heart 19
What is it about? 22
Ring in the season of peace 25
The light of compassion 27
Mommy and I are one 29
The pregnant man 30
You are so powerful 31
Circles of compassion 32
The journey is your mirror 35
I will be true 37
As above, so below 38

The children are coming 39
The Seeing Eye (1) 40
The Seeing Eye (2) 41
The Seeing Eye (3) 42
The Seeing Eye (4) 43
Consciousness 44
Relativity 45
Every day is winter 47

PART III   SOUL STIRRINGS

Weaverbirds 51
Night critters play 52
The eerie guild 54
Chicago at night 56
Paris 57
Seattle 58

PART IV   RISING DOWN THE LADDER

Death at old age 61
Alehah hashalom 63
Ascension 64
I shall not fear 65
A mighty canoe has sunk 66
Like seagulls 68
Is it true what they say? 69

I

Lovers play hide and seek

A lover getting ready

You have long been ready, my Love
Waiting so patiently for me to be willing.
You know how it feels when one lover is ready
And the other is not.

But you continued to wait
Knowing that someday,
I would be ready.

At last I have kicked off my dirty shoes of guilt,
I am getting ready for you.
I have discarded my clothes of pride
I am getting ready for you.
I have slipped off my undergarments of fear
I am getting ready for you.
I am getting ready…

Now I am totally ready,
Free in my nothingness
Willing to come to you,
You who waited so long
For me to be ready.

I am now ready for you, my Love!

January 17, 2003.

All I want is love, love, love

Something is happening inside me
Right where my heart beats
It feels as if I'm in love

(Who doesn't like that feeling?)
It seems as if nothing else matters
And it surely feels good.
It feels as if I'm in love

I wonder how I can feel this peace
When all around me battles rage?
I wonder how I can feel this love
When hatred and prejudice tear about me.

I wonder how I can feel this joy
When pain and sorrow swirl around?
But I cannot deny what I feel
Right where my heart beats.

All I want to do
Is love, love, love
And all I want to be now
Is love, love, love.

I want to love the life about me
And the essence of my roots.

I want to love those who love me
And those who don't.

All I want to do now
Is love, love, love
And all I want to be now
Is love, love, love.

I want to love those who cherish me
And those who reject me.
I want to love those who extol the divine in me
And those who deny my humanity.

All I want to do now
Is love, love, love
And all I want to be now
Is love, love, love.

I want to love those who appreciate me
And those who don't
I want to love those who treat me justly
And those who don't.

All I want to do now
Is love, love, love
And all I want to be now
Is love, love, love.

I want to love the rose
And its thorns.
I want to love the honey
And the bee stings.
I want to love the placid sea
And its tempests.

Ready for your love

All I want to do now
Is love, love, love
And all I want to be now
Is love, love, love.

I want to love the Sun, the heat
The Moon, the dark.
I want to love the dangerous snake
And I want to love the dove.

Because something is happening inside me
Right where my heart beats
I sense an awesome change
Right within me.

And all I want to experience now
Is love, love, love
And all I want to be
Is love, love, love.

January 25, 2003

Ineffable love

Why, my Love, do you shower me
With such sweetness that blows away
My mind? Unworthiness was all

I heard and saw and knew and felt
As the real me before you came
Into my life even as I
Was not all that ready for your love.
I haven't offered you diamonds or
Dear jewelry made from gold or
Exotic stones like tanzanite;

No silver bands, no wooden rings,
No incense offerings and
No giving of flowers; I have
Offered you no wine and I have
Offered no sumptuous meals, offered
You not even a glass of water.

Still, still….still you find me
Trustworthy and lovable.

You did not exact promises
From me, no conditions
And you slipped softly into my

Ready for your love

Heart, making a home for yourself
There in my heart overflowing
Now with the sweetness of your love.

How, my Love, have you transformed
My fearful horse into one of courage
My vengeful army into this
Delegation of peace, and my
Barren lands into oases of life?
How, my Love, did you do that?

You shower me with such sweetness:
You find me trustworthy, lovable
You did not exact promises
From me, no conditions
You simply slipped into my heart
Even as I was not all that
Ready for your all-accepting love.
Why, my Love, do you shower me
With such sweetness that blows away
My mind? Why, my Love?

January 14, 2003

Numinous lovers play hide and seek (1)

My Love, You are so funny!
You like to play hide and seek with me.
You are somewhere in the gardens
Surrounding this house
Or you are inside the house
Where you are hiding from me,
Giggling in silence
So I cannot find you.
I look for you outside,
In this garden with blooms
In which nectar-sucking bees buzz,
Where butterflies make love in the air,
Where birds feast on ripe fruits
Scenting the fresh air.
I look for you in trees
With burdened branches,
Where playful squirrels
Steal away fruits
Lying on the ground.

Numinous lovers play hide and seek (2)

Where are you, my Love?
Love, are you hiding
Behind the flowers...
Or have you climbed a tree—
To hide in its green leaves
Glistening with water droplets
As you munch a luscious fruit?
Do you cross your fingers
That I should not see you?

Numinous lovers play hide and seek (3)

Where can I find you, my Love?
I look through curtains
I peep through keyholes
Thinking you will stand carelessly
So I can pull a fast one on you.
But you are adept
At your game of hide and seek
I cannot find you so easily.

I open the door and enter
I dart straight to the basement.
It's dark in here.
Wait! I think I hear your steps!
I flip on the light, but you are not here.
I turn off the light, and I climb the stairs

Looking for you in all the obvious places,
On all the floors of this huge house
I call my home, my Inner Castle.

Numinous lovers play hide and seek (4)

In effervescent desolation I throw myself
On this velvet-covered bed
Vanilla and ocean scented.
I catch reflections of flowers
On the window, and then…

You jump on me; you press
Your lips against my lips. Your
Electrifying breath tingles my body.
Together we roll on the bed.
You laugh and you tell me
That all along you had tiptoed behind me,
Praying that I would turn
To find you—but I never turned.
And I said, Love, your name is Funny.
I am so glad you at last let me find you.
I could never have discovered you on my own
Because you are so very good
At your game of hide and seek—
And you do wear that cloak of invisibility.

January 20, 2003

Committing to Spirit

Funny and silly this is:
But whoever has flirted with you
Knows that you are, Beloved Spirit,
The embodiment
Of exuberance and joy.

So humor me when I say
This day I thee wed.

And here is my marriage vow to you:
I promise to be grateful for your love
And never to take it for granted.

I promise that I will always confess
That I am naive,
Innocent of your ways.
But I am willing to learn
Through all the means
By which you teach Life's lessons
Because to know your ways
Is to grow in your love.

For your sake, I choose to tell
The truth that I know and feel
That I may be congruent
In body, mind, and spirit.

Ready for your love

I am choosing peace:
Nurturing whoever, whatever, fosters peace
Above all else:
Because of your love for me.

I cherish my freedom.
I allow others to be free
And responsible for their choices
As I honor you, Spirit, the source of my being.

For your love, Spirit, I choose moderation
In my thoughts, feelings, actions.

I choose to love and serve others
The best way I can,
Because only in loving others
Can I give meaning to the love
That you have for me.
I choose to do what I am
In the vehicles I now possess
And I surrender my efforts,
Trials, and successes to you.

Beloved Spirit, I will not agonize
Over how I can keep my promises
Because I know that it is my sincere commitment
That matters to you.

And I know that no matter what I do
And no matter what I say
You will find it funny and silly
Because I am naïve,
Innocent of your ways

Kwami E. Nyamidie

But all I have to do
Is open my heart to your love.
All I have to do
Is open my heart to your love.

March 13, 2003.

Compassion

It builds in my heart
Like clouds over land.
Dispersed thought vapors
Unite and form concrete
Acts of compassion
Falling on mankind
Like heavy downpour
In a season of drought.

December 2002.

II

Egg in a tornado eye

You all are in my heart

Beloved, you ring in my heart
Sublime harmony of
Chiming music oozing from
Universal keys.

Parents and siblings, friends,
Co-workers, old classmates, and all
You who once knew my name
Who once cast your eyes on me
Like sun rays falling on a mirror
Passengers in cars, buses,
Trains and planes.

You are in my heart
Endless water dripping trickles
In a serene waterfall
Whispering softly in my heart.

You are in my heart:
Childhood friends
Forced to exit
Before you acted your apparent roles
In life's drama,
Too soon.

And you older folks
Tired of living, praying

Ready for your love

For the coming of the reaper.
You, too, are in my heart.

You are in my heart:
Heroes and warriors
All you teachers and masters
Great minds and leaders
Who ever walked this earth;
You rest in my heart.

And you are in my heart too:
Slaves buried in unmarked graves
Executed traitors and murderers
Whose spirits roam restlessly
In the dark, cold, lonely underworld,
Waiting for the day the chains will break,
Waiting for the liberating light.
You struggle here in my heart, playing
Life's harmony-sustaining chords.

You are in my heart: sweet honey
From nectar, you are in my heart;
Bitter dregs from medicine leaves,
You are in my heart, creeping critters
And chirping birds, you mountain peaks
And ocean depths, you wetlands
And desert places;
You are all in my heart.

You are in my heart,
Fixed stars with changing colors
Visible and invisible heavenly bodies
Of day and night.

Kwami E. Nyamidie

All you are in my heart
Unique instruments of the symphony
Whose music I hear in the soul of my soul
In the heart of my heart

December 27, 2002

What is it about?

It's not about
competition
money
power
fame
sex
the body
or death.

It's not about
pain
fear
sorrow
hatred
or despair.

It's not about the mind—
thinking
dreaming
analyzing
or doubting.

It's about
The voice in us that speaks,
The power in us that sees,
tastes
hears

smells
perceives.

It's about The Presence.
It's about
This Ocean of Life
of which we are droplets.

This holographic universe
in our heart.
It's about compassion,
The love that binds all created things,
The love that unites all people
from all races and places
and brings them together
in a place like this.

It's about the love
that feels this Presence
In the high and the lowly
in the rich and the poor
in the famous and the dejected
in the beloved and the hated.

That's what this is all about:
Unmasking and
Glorifying Spirit
In all its guises.

And it is this I am grateful for
This very day,
This very hour,

Ready for your love

This very moment,
Here.

November 28, 2002

Ring in the season of peace
For Christmas.

Christmas day:
This is the season of peace
But the specter of war
Dangles like a Damocles sword

This is the season of love
But the dark clouds from the aura of hatred
Cover the face of the Earth
Blocking the light of peace.

The clamor of arms on the battlefield
The wailing of widows and orphan babies
Suffocate the carols in the places of worship

The carrion stench
Of fallen soldiers out smell
The sweet-smelling incense

The irony of Santa Claus fantasy
Betrays ignorance of our predicament.
Every day Gaia bleeds
Her children are brutalized

Through war, sickness, and poverty.
There is no wooden manger this time
Where the savior of mankind may nestle.

Ready for your love

The Savior has chosen to be born
Into the stillness of the ready heart
Unfettered by the transient clutter
Of our arrogant egos.

Oh, the magnitude of courage it takes
So the Savior can be born
Into the quiet of the heart
In the middle of all this turmoil

(Like an egg a hen lays
In a tornado eye)
Into the turbulent consciousness
That harbors the heart's delicate manger

This is the time to ring in the season of peace
To ring in the season of love
Into the sacred stillness of our heart
Into the manger within

Where the Inner Savior may be born
That war may be banished
And hatred vanquished.

December 19, 2002.

The light of compassion
For Christmas, 2003.

They say I can see
That I can behold the Light.

They say a lighthouse guides us
across life's dark and tumultuous seas.

But like a blind man
on a storm-tossed ship,
I walk the deck, groping
In the darkness covering me.

"What is all this talk of light about?"

I know not glittering diamonds,
rainbows, fireflies,
bushes burning in dry plains,
sunlight flickering on fallen snows.

In vain I hear of the light of a sunrise,
Of shooting stars falling in a moonless night.

In vain I hear of Venus rising
Of Saturn setting.

Tell me not of any Light.

I am sorry.

Ready for your love

I cannot see,
My eyes cannot see.

But let me know
one act of your compassion,
of your understanding,
of your forgiveness,
and Light floods into my eyes,
and I see an Infinite brightness:

A Light even I,
A blind seeker with eyes shut,
can see:

And I know
This Light is God

And your love
Opens my inner eyes to a Light
That even the blind can see.

And I know that this light
is that Light that shines
across life's vast ocean
over which we sail
through this mystery of our lives
and which brings us to safe harbor
and returns us to our true home.

December 22, 2003.

Mommy and I are one

From nowhere you carried me
In your body
In the warmth of your inside
The comfort of a well-heated winter home
In your womb.

With your life you shielded me
For more than nine months
I did not want to leave
The safety of your protection.

Too soon, I had to go
Into the bitter coldness of the outside
Too soon, away
From the ocean of your love.

After these several winters gone by
I still dream of returning
Into the soothing warmth
Of your inside
Oh Mother
Because I am one with you.

May 6, 1996.
Washington, DC.

The pregnant man

I am a pregnant man
Curled up inside
Laboring day to day
To set myself free
From the narrow world of my womb
From the world that covers me.

I am a chrysalis
Struggling second after second
To set myself free
And move about unrestricted
A butterfly in the air.

I am a bird in a cage
Groping night in, night out
To find that gate
That at last shall set me free
To fly over land and sea.

I am a pregnant man
Curled up inside
Fighting day to day
To set myself free.

You are so powerful

How are you so powerful,
Gentleness that lives in my heart?
You are like the serene breeze
That spreads over quiet ocean shores
With the diffused scent of a lonely rose
Barely perceptible.

You are the fading echo
Of giggling bells
Fine dew droplets at dawn
And the first rays of
Life seed bearing sunlight
At daybreak.

How then are you so powerful,
Gentleness that lives in my heart?
You who are like the quiet rustle
Of life in a baby cuddling
Against my chest?

You are the all-present
Foundation on which I stand
The foundation on which
The entire universe spins.
Gentleness that lives in my heart
You are so powerful.

January 13, 2003.

Circles of compassion

All around me
cries for help
go unspoken.
Not victims faraway—

but persons near at hand—
family and friends and the stranger
near at hand—like me—
Are joined in silence—

forbidden to express their need.
Can someone hear them?
A single mother struggling
to educate her teens

calls for help, silently.
A man loses his job
and is too embarrassed
to speak
As I pass him
on my way to work

He calls for help, silently.
A couple wondering
how love and life
Can be so hard

call out for help,
silently.

A child struggles
with challenges too great
for her few years
is calling for help,
silently.

Justice denied in
the corridors of power
is calling out for help.

Lovers of Peace
surrounded by
deserts of violence
cry out for help
Do you hear these cries?
Listen carefully.

Do you hear
the sound of caring
in the beating
of our hearts?

That is Earth's music
we are meant to sing
in this place,
in our midst.

Listen to the sound of caring,
listen to the Earth's song
we are meant to sing
here and now.

Ready for your love

May we unite
in circles of compassion
in communities of hope
and free ourselves
of the prison of indifference.

Feb 2, 2003.

The journey is your mirror

For Jeannine Daggett
On Coming Back From Africa.

Before you set out on your journey
Pull out the maps
But first dust off your mirror:
Look into your face, then plan
Where you want to go.

Look right into the mirror, harder
What you see there is what
You'll get on your journey;
What escapes you now
Will seek you out,
Unsolicited.

Look into your mirror
Before you set out on your journey.
You cast your reflections
In the shadows of self-knowledge
Wherever you go!

When you take a walk in the woods
Forget winter, forget summer;
Forget spring and forget fall!
Your changing self

Ready for your love

Your changeless Self
Reveal your seasons.

Look, therefore, into the still pool.
What you see in the valley
Is what you'll find
At the mountaintop.

And when you return,
Listen to the stories that you tell
You found only yourself
Your journey was your mirror!

November 20 2003.
Kwami E. Nyamidie.

I will be true

I will listen to the Voice
Despite everything else I hear all day
I will be true to myself
No matter what others say.

To Spirit I will be true
When the Me the Others betray.

I will be true, I will be true
Because you give me joy
I will be true.
Because you give me peace
I will be true.

I will listen to the voice
Despite everything else I hear all day
I will be true to myself
No matter what others say.

I will be true, I will be true
I will be true to the Spirit
That lives in me.

January 13, 2003

As above, so below

My eyes are fixed on things on high
on mysteries of galaxies and nebulae
on planets guiding my steps below.
My eyes are fixed on Hale-Bopp
A comet Pharaohs saw
When they built their pyramids.

Like Cheops I, too, am building a pyramid.
An inner one, but still a pyramid,
A great and awesome monument
As I look inside the vast untapped
Resources trapped and buried
In the soul of my soul.

I look up in awe and wonder
And I see within and below the mystery
That I am, the mystery of mud
Transforming itself daily, slowly into gold;
The mystery of the edifice I construct
Painfully and surely with each stone
Of life's experience.

March 24, 1997.

The children are coming

The children are coming,
Are coming,
The children of the Water Bearer
Are coming
To steal our thirst away.

The children are coming,
Are coming,
The Children of the Light
Are coming
To cast our darkness away.

The Seeing Eye (1)

New moon and full moon
New year and birthdays
Spin on the wheel of time
Winter flows into spring
Summer turns into fall

I am the Seeing Eye
Looking as the wheel spins
On Eternity's axis.

December 31, 2001.

The Seeing Eye (2)

I am the Seeing Eye
Watching as I grow
In my mother's womb
Looking on as I learn to crawl
As I take my faltering steps.

I am the Seeing Eye
Watching my stuttering lips
Utter my first words.

Countless haircuts later
And baskets of fingernails pared
The cells of my body
Are renewed

But I remain the same.

December 31, 2001.

The Seeing Eye (3)

Like a bottle with a message
Floating on the oceans
Drifting on icebergs
I swim with sharks and dolphins
In the tropical seas at midnight
Where shooting stars
Draw streaks of white light
Across the canvas of darkness
The tempestuous seas hurl me
Against the waves

Still I float
A message in the bottle
Written in hieroglyphics
Reads:
I am the Seeing Eye.

December 31, 2001

The Seeing Eye (4)

I am the Seeing Eye
I am the Knowing Eye.

January 1, 2002.

Consciousness

Consciousness,
My night consciousness,
Where do you leave me
When I sleep at night

When other mysterious dramas unfold?
I shall no more permit you
My waking consciousness,
To drop me dead like lead on my bed.

Tonight I shall not be content
With ephemeral pleasures
I shall cling with you
So we can sail together to worlds

Beyond this world.
Be my guide at night
As you have been to me in the day
Faithful companion of awareness

Forsake me not
In this world of sleep
Where I shall perceive life
With new eyes.

Relativity
For Melissa K. Helmenstine

Sunrise in spring and the birds sing
Their love songs. Flowers bloom
Snow has melted, darkness gone.
Laughter flows from the heart.

Yonder, on the other side,
Autumn leaves fall, looms
Dreary and cold winter. Harvest time
Has come, harvest time is gone.

Sunrise here, sunset there
Birth for some, death for others.

Dreams come true now turn seeds
For another harvest
An exit opens the door—
Enter.

We weave life's web
With threads of going in and coming out
We play in life's symphony
Syncopated silence and sound
Of endings and beginnings
Sunrise here and sunset there

Ready for your love

As love birds in spring
Forget the dreary cold of winter.

April 21, 2002.

Every day is winter

Every day is winter:
Fall is winter,
Spring is winter,
Even summer is winter
In the world of Spirit.

Everything in the Spirit
Looks like snow:
Man-made creations from clay, stone
Wood, ivory, bronze, iron,
Silver, gold;
Creatures like birds and fishes,
Mammals and trees
Are snow
And the spirit merges with all things—
Like fog and snowflakes,
Hovering over primordial stuff.

Everything is snow
And we are the snowmen
Creating our own realities
With our imagination.

Because
Every day is winter,
Spring is winter,

Ready for your love

Even summer is winter
In the world of Spirit.

Spirit pervades everything
Like melting foggy snowflakes
And we are snowmen
Wearing the warm winter clothes
Of sacred knowledge that
Energy follows thought:
And with our minds
We create our world!

December 17, 2002

III

Soul stirrings

Weaverbirds

Faithful to oaths they swore to nature
At the rise of life, weaverbirds
Busy themselves building their nests
From sunrise to sunset. Their market-day
Noises make deaf ears hear.

Firmly hooked on their beaks hang
Shooting star trails of weeds torn
From haggard looking palm trees
That wave their tattered
Feathery fronds in the breeze.

Their rhythmic thrusts, short firefly dashes,
Like light calabashes that float on water
Keep them weightless up in the air.

Disarmed snakes and hawks pry about powerless
Marveling at the weed fortresses of the weaverbirds.
Strong tree-uprooting winds blew
Unhurt remain the nests these birds built
Rains driving rats from holes came
Undrenched the sagacious weaverbirds.

Night critters play

The night sky glows with the light from the moon
The pupa curls up in her cozy cocoon.
Shimmering stars dot the sky and Milky Way
While night birds and critters slip out to play.
Big-eyed owls sing songs to the nightly sky,
Hoo, hoo, friends, come out now and watch us fly.
From tadpole-filled ponds frogs croak their own chants:
Anthems to branches of tall jungly plants.
Moonlit bugs hop in manners most proper:
Scratching out calls some hundreds of crickets
Ask friends to play with them in the thickets:
Let's go, praying mantis; come, grasshopper.
With night as her cover, the gray armadillo
Shoots a quick glance from her leaf-packed pillow.
Thorny brothers under their skin,
The hedgehog and the porcupine
Sniff out the nighttime spot they're in
Looking for some quiet space to dine.
They know they are safe now from dangerous light.
With eagles moon-banished and vultures at bay,
Jungle creatures jump and crawl into the night
They don't know the reason; it's just Nature's way.
Under night's dark shield critters surge, move, and hop:
Bugs flit, fireflies glow, snails slide, owls soar on top
In the water, crabs crawl, fishes leap, flip
While prickly shore critters take their night trip.

Then...
The lion roars,
The crocodile barks and
All is quiet.
Frightened, crabs crawl back into holes deep
Frogs hop out the ponds; into holes in trees
Armadillos climb in the dawn breeze
And the night's playing creatures must rush to sleep.
The Milky Way loses all her freckles
The drowsy leopard stretches her speckles
The sky lightens; a day critter stirs in a nest,
The moon slips to her invisible bed to rest...

September 2002.

The eerie guild

At dead of night, they leave their loved ones
To meet under dreaded trees where
They plan and swear to bring unborn babies
And drink human blood.

Slouching out of their numb bodies
Like snakes discarding out-grown skins,
They dive, human frogs living on the dry land
Of the physical world, in the water of spirit life
They dive deep into boundless sea.
Here, fragile matter shatters,
Crumbles, dissolves like smoke
Scattered in the air. Here, all is shifting,
Fleeting, unsteady, distorted:
Floating images on a television screen.

There they go at night,
Plunging into the etheric seas
To swim, play, feast with handsome men, fair ladies,
Half-human, fish tail, curling fairy hair
Covering golden breasts, diamond sparkling eyes.
There they go at mid-night, flying like birds
Embracing winged crocodiles, pythons with claws,
Seven-headed serpents dancing to music
From flutes and reeds.

Kwami E. Nyamidie

They go there at dead of night
Destroying, interfering with archetypes
And pleasurable events yet to materialize
In lives of innocent victims sleeping
In a sleepless world.

Chicago at night

Beads of sparkling diamonds
Sprawling on a canvas of darkness

Feb 24, 2002.

Paris,

efflorescence nourished
by the martyrs' blood.

Seattle

You stir my soul with fear
As though I stand on holy ground.
An uneasy solemn-ness pervades your lakes
And streams, reminding me
Of my childhood dreams.

Are you the sunset
Of man's civilization

Rising at dawn in the East with Confucius,
Passing the morning over India,
Over Egypt and its pyramids
While Jesus walked the shores of Galilee
At civilization's mid-day?

Seattle, are you the setting of the old world
Soon to go the way of Athens and Rome,
Lisbon and London?
I think I saw it pass the zenith in D.C.
And it is now here
In Seattle.

Are you then, Seattle, on the cusp of
The dawn of a new age?

Tell me,
Seattle.

1996

IV

Rising down the ladder

Death at old age
For Willfried F. Feuser
1928–2000

You dog me like a shadow
This bright desert summer day.

At sunrise your disproportionate height
Dwarfs and reminds me
Of your haunting presence,
Constantly.

Mid-life comes at mid-day
As I beat my chest,
Raise my fist
And dare you to a duel.

But you hide from me
As I glow in the halo of eternity
The sweet sap of life intoxicates me
I feel I live forever.

Alas
Slowly, quietly,
The years roll by
And from your eclipsed size at noon
You emerge beneath me
Growing bigger, mightier,
Swallowing me in the darkness

Ready for your love

At sunset
In the powerless night
Of my silent grave.

[Seattle, Washington, USA
July 21, 2000.]

Alehah hashalom

For Tutu Lee Alhadeff
1925–2000

How this Egg of mine
Has survived that long
Amazes me.

Countless times has it fallen on stone
Countless times was it saved from breaking

Weep not, weep not for me,
Now that my life's egg is crushed
And the essence of my being
Spills out, lost for awhile to you
But fused within my Maker,
The timeless unbreakable receptacle
For the essence of my being
Wrapped in the indestructible shroud
Of my Creator,
In my everlasting home.

August 15, 2000

Ascension

For Peter Ifedapo Feuser

I peep down the ladder
and watch myself
through memory's dim mirror
vomited out of the sea
greeting the world in sorrow
while the hosts welcome me
in tears of joy.

You raise your gaze above the ladder
and behold them hurl you
down the pit unwillingly
while your tired soul
rejoices in the solace
of the long-awaited respite.

We are rising down a ladder
ascending below life
beneath the earth
to be trampled and
trampled on.

I shall not fear
For Peter Ifedapo Feuser

Fear, I shall not fear
the warped reflections
on memory's silvery waves.

Nor shall I incessantly fear
the haunting echo
yelling out of consciousness'
abysmal cave.

Will no more perturb me
the dazzling lightning
of intuition rending asunder
perception's dark robe.

Fear, I shall no more fear
speculations on the solemn shaft's
obscure terrain where shall
lie vanquished this clay clod
the cold, discarded cocoon
of a butterfly spinning,
boundless, freely,
in eternity's sea.

A mighty canoe has sunk
For Professor Edith Ihekweazu 1941–1991

Listen to the jarring noises I hear
Cats I see mewing at noon
While black dogs bark at strange sights.
O look, look at the serpent
Drying itself across my way, motionless.
Above me hover bats
In broad daylight.

My head is weighed down
By an invisible stone
I shiver with prickly skin
Does dew fall at noon?

Che-e-e-e!
The mighty bridge across
The Niger has collapse
U-u-u-i-i-e!
The mail van is drowned!

See ripples of jarring noises
on the boisterous river
smell the strong stench
of cat excreta in the shadows
while dogs still bark at bats at noon
And the green snake sleeps across my path
For a mighty canoe has sunk

Kwami E. Nyamidie

A mighty canoe has sunk
Into the Niger river
Into the deep river.
August 6, 1992.

Like seagulls

In the twilight of the setting sun, I watch
From my plane the charming sea kissing
The golden coast with its long lips of waves.
Beyond as far as my eyes can stretch
Seagulls fly like me to an unknown land,
Towards somewhere across the sea,
Beyond my life's sea: the scene clears off
From my view, too soon. Like a sly robber
Death waylays me; infinity surrounds me—
A serpent; eternity wraps me with
A doomed cloth. And, like the aimless seagulls, I
Fly towards an ultimate and unknown destination
Towards the land of no return…

Port Harcourt, May 1990.

Is it true what they say?

They say some day
I will see you face to face.
Do you actually have a face?

And they say someday
I will hear your voice.
Do you really have a voice?

They say some day
You will well up in my heart
Like a spring that will never go dry.
Who will dig the well?

Can it be that I see your face
Every day in some form
Unknown to me?

Or can it be that I hear your voice
Every day in some way
Without recognizing it is you?

Can it be that you are
Always in my heart,
Unaware to me
You are there?

Is it true that someday I will
Actually see you face-to-face,
That someday I will

Ready for your love

Really hear your voice,
That someday I will
Stand before my heart's well
And drink from this spring
That does not go dry?

Is it true what they say?
"You must find out for yourself,"
I think I hear the Voice say.

January 20, 2003

0-595-30643-8

CPSIA information can be obtained
at www.ICGtesting.com
Printed in the USA
FSOW03n1459070617
34945FS